See Something, Say Something

Joe Rhatigan

Reader Consultants

Jennifer M. Lopez, M.S.Ed., NBCT
Senior Coordinator—History/Social Studies
Norfolk Public Schools

Tina Ristau, M.A., SLMS
Teacher Librarian
Waterloo Community School District

iCivics Consultants

Emma Humphries, Ph.D.
Chief Education Officer

Taylor Davis, M.T.
Director of Curriculum and Content

Natacha Scott, MAT
Director of Educator Engagement

Publishing Credits

Rachelle Cracchiolo, M.S.Ed., *Publisher*
Emily R. Smith, M.A.Ed., *VP of Content Development*
Véronique Bos, *Creative Director*
Dona Herweck Rice, *Senior Content Manager*
Dani Neiley, *Associate Content Specialist*
Fabiola Sepulveda, *Series Designer*

Image Credits: All images from iStock and/or Shutterstock

Library of Congress Cataloging-in-Publication Data

Names: Rhatigan, Joe, author.
Title: See something, say something / Joe Rhatigan.
Description: Huntington Beach, CA : Teacher Created Materials, [2021] | Includes index. | Audience: Grades 2-3 | Summary: "Sometimes things that look bad but aren't. Other times, it is better to speak up. But how do you know when to say something?"-- Provided by publisher.
Identifiers: LCCN 2020043568 (print) | LCCN 2020043569 (ebook) | ISBN 9781087605029 (paperback) | ISBN 9781087620046 (ebook)
Subjects: LCSH: Threat (Psychology)--Juvenile literature. | Danger perception--Juvenile literature. | Children and adults--Juvenile literature.
Classification: LCC BF575.T45 R53 2021 (print) | LCC BF575.T45 (ebook) | DDC 155.9--dc23
LC record available at https://lccn.loc.gov/2020043568
LC ebook record available at https://lccn.loc.gov/2020043569

TCM Teacher Created Materials
5482 Argosy Avenue
Huntington Beach, CA 92649-1039
www.tcmpub.com

ISBN 978-1-0876-0502-9

Table of Contents

You Can Make a Difference

We spend a lot of time with other people. We play, go to school, and hang out with friends and family. It can be fun. But there can be times when things **confuse** us. Sometimes we see things that might make us **uncomfortable**, scared, or angry. It is important to know that you can help make a difference. And it starts with knowing when to say something.

Jump into Fiction

Brian's Decision

Brian is leaving school. He sees his friend Angelica and waves hello. A strange man gets out of a car and approaches Angelica. He starts talking to her. The man is not Angelica's dad. Brian knows it's not safe to talk to strangers, but should he do something?

Brian thinks. *Should I go up to them? Maybe I should yell something. Or… maybe I shouldn't say anything at all.*

Brian runs back inside the school. He tells his teacher, Mr. Arnold, what he saw. Mr. Arnold heads outside. Brian feels like maybe he did something wrong. Mr. Arnold comes back. He tells Brian there is nothing to worry about.

"That's Angelica's uncle," he says.

Brian feels bad. "Did I do something wrong? Should I have minded my own business?"

Mr. Arnold says, "You did the right thing! Everything was fine. But you helped me keep Angelica safe. It is always better to be safe than sorry."

Back to Nonfiction

A Small Act

See something, say something. That's a popular saying. But what does it mean? It means that if you see something bad going on, tell an adult. If you feel that something is wrong, tell an adult.

It can also mean looking out for others. Maybe you see a kid being bullied. You could be nice to them instead. Maybe you see a kid sitting alone at lunch. You could sit with them. Sometimes a small act can make a big difference.

Left Out

Some people might feel left out. They might be alone often. They might feel sad or even mad about it. A small act, such as asking if they want to sit with you at lunch, can mean a lot.

When You See Something

It is not always easy to tell if something is wrong. Even if you are not sure, it is best to tell an adult. Maybe nothing is wrong. That's totally fine! It is better to be safe than sorry. It's an adult's job to make sure everything is okay. You can help them do that. Speaking up is one of the best ways to help.

Talking to an adult can be helpful.

Who Can You Talk To?

Who is a good adult to talk to? It should be an adult you trust. That might be a parent. It might be a teacher, a police officer, or a family friend.

Scary things can happen. Sometimes you might not be sure what is going on. There might even be times when there isn't anything wrong. No one seems to be in **danger** or is getting hurt. But something might seem weird or wrong anyway. Maybe an adult you don't know has been hanging around the playground. You have a bad feeling. Find the nearest adult you can trust and tell them.

Talking to adults you trust is always a good idea.

What Is "Stranger Danger"?

"Stranger danger" means to stay away from and not **approach** people you don't know. Most teachers are adults who can be trusted.

Bullying

Imagine that two of your friends are joking together. They call each other names. Do you need to say something? If both friends know they are **teasing** and no one is hurt by it, then you probably don't need to say anything. But if one person feels hurt by it, then it is not okay. You should say something to the friend who was mean.

Teasing can hurt people's feelings.

What if you hear a friend call someone mean names every day? What if they leave that person out of games on purpose or hurt them? Should you say something? Yes! This is called **bullying**. And bullying is hurtful.

When Is It Bullying?

Bullying can come in different forms. It can be mean words or names. It can be pushing or shoving. If you see something that seems wrong, say something.

Siblings often tattle on each other.

Is It Tattling?

Have you ever been told to stop **tattling**? You might wonder if telling an adult that someone is doing a bad thing is tattling. This can be confusing. How do you know when it is okay to say something?

Ask yourself this: Could someone be in danger? Maybe your brother eats dessert before dinner. Is anyone in danger? No. So it is not your job to tell.

Now, think about if you saw a kid at school write a note that says he will hit another kid. Someone might be in danger. Now it is your job to tell.

It's OK to tell a teacher if someone is in danger.

Do not tell on someone just to get them in trouble. Only tell an adult if someone might be in danger. So, your friend says they are going to run away. Is it okay to tell an adult? Yes! Running away is definitely not safe. Your friend may be angry with you for telling. But you helped them stay safe, and that's important.

Think and Talk

How do you know you can trust a person?

Feeling Bad

Sometimes, you might feel bad for speaking up. You might feel like you did something wrong. Or maybe you're afraid of getting someone else in trouble. You might not want to tell an adult. But not saying anything might make it worse.

Think and Talk

Why did the author choose to include this photo in the book?

Let's say you see a friend being mean to another kid in your class. You want to tell your teacher. But you feel bad about it because they are your friend. You don't want to make your friend **upset**. You should talk to your teacher. It is always best to do the right thing.

Always Look Out

Making sure people are safe is important. When something feels wrong, let an adult know. If a friend or someone else could get hurt, tell an adult you trust. Keep in mind that it is better to be safe than sorry.

Scary things happen. But there are people around to help. You can help too. Be watchful. And don't be afraid to speak up. Remember, if you see something, say something.

Glossary

approach—move closer

bullying—when someone stronger or more powerful mistreats someone else

confuse—to make something hard to understand

danger—something that may cause injury, pain, or loss

tattling—telling someone about what someone else has done

teasing—annoying or making fun of

uncomfortable—feeling discomfort

upset—troubled by something

Index

Civics in Action

Leaders are helpful and kind. They help in difficult situations. Anyone can be helpful. You just need to look for opportunities to help. One way to be a leader is by being a friend. Get involved in a Friend Patrol!

1. Start a Friend Patrol at your school. Invite other kids to join.
2. Look for kids who are sad, alone, or picked on.
3. Be friendly. Say hello.
4. Ask kids who seem shy or lonely if they want to play or have lunch with you.
5. Help make a big difference in someone's life!